Stoned, Naked and Looking in my Neighbour's Window

Stoned, Naked and Looking in my Neighbour's Window

compiled by
Gabriel Jeffrey
creator of GroupHug.us

SIMON &
SCHUSTER

First published in Great Britain by Simon & Schuster UK Ltd, 2004
A Viacom company

1 3 5 7 9 10 8 6 4 2

Simon & Schuster UK Ltd
Africa House · 64-78 Kingsway · London WC2B 6AH

www.simonsays.co.uk

Simon & Schuster Australia · Sydney

A CIP catalogue record for this book is
available from the British Library

ISBN 0-7432-6826-1
EAN 9780743268264

Text design by Lovelock & Co.
Printed and bound in Great Britain by
Mackays of Chatham plc

'It is the confession, not the priest, that gives us absolution'
Oscar Wilde

"Their beauty is their confession."
- St. Augustine

The best experiences of your life are the
ones when you're not a customer. When there
is no product, no value-proposition.
Swimming in the ocean. Eating berries from
a vine. Screwing without a condom. It was
these sentiments, and the inevitability of
their co-option by Diesel and Volkswagen,
that got me thinking about a new project.
The heart of it would be anonymity, which
is terribly undervalued. If you're at a
party giving out business cards, nobody's

writing songs about you. Go to a rock show and buy drinks for strangers, they'll remember you. People tell better stories to strangers.

When it came to the context and the format, it seemed sort of obvious. Confession - whether once a week in a booth to a priest, or once a week in a civic building to a bunch of fellow alcoholics - has this sacred, candid, alarmingly visceral meaning to a lot of people. Calling these anonymous stories confessions would require very little further explanation. I wanted to collect stories about weakness, rage, affairs, desperation, fetishes, and all the other really human things that don't belong on an earnings report. The truth is that most jobs suck, being fat and spoiled doesn't make kids happy, your girlfriend might have been thinking about someone else last night, the kid at the burger place probably will spit in your food if you're a dick to him.

So on October 1, 2003 I posted the first confession, a simple one:

469666749
I normally do not smoke, but when I am really stressed out about something I can comfortably smoke nearly a pack a day.

And posted a link to my blog.* For several days it was an intimate little site that only a few people knew about; a big game of

* gabrieljeffrey.com/log.

truth or dare or something, like having friends out on the small back porch of my apartment. That metaphor got flimsy in the second week and by week three the porch would have caved in, killing and maiming hundreds - there were more than 2.5 million pages served up that week.

In February 2004 I went to Austin, Texas, to work on another project. On a walk to get coffee one morning through a South Austin neighborhood, my mobile phone rang and showed a blocked number.

"Hello?"

"Mr. Jeffrey?"

"Yes."

"Is this Mr. Gabriel Jeffrey."

"Yes, this is Mr. Gabriel Jeffrey."

"Do you own grouphug.us?"

"Yup."

"This is the Secret Service."

"Okay."

"We're concerned about a note on your Web site. We would like to contact the individual who wrote this note. Can you help us contact the individual who wrote this note?"

"No."

"There's no way to contact the individual?"

"No, the site is anonymous. There's no way to contact them."

"Anonymous? Can you please explain how it's anonymous?"

"Well, the server keeps no visitor logs. Um, all we record is the date, the text they type, and a random number."

"A random number?"

"A random number."

"Okay. Thank you."

"Wait. What did the confession say?"

"It threatened the life of the President of the United States."

"Oh, okay. Bye."

That's the story I tell when someone asks me how I guarantee anonymity. If the United States Secret Service is satisfied, well, some of those guys are pretty smart. They all look like they must have MBAs or something. And their phone voices are hot.

I started compiling this book in the spring of 2004. After months of reading confessions, they really all start to look the same. It made it impossible to find the "best" confessions, which of course is relative to begin with. My approach became to find the most representative confessions, to distill tens of thousands of pages of personal confessions into a palpable document. There are no points for spelling and grammar online, which means that I had a hard choice to make in the editing of this book. One of my favorite examples of a typical submission:

160342055
i found out somthing that feels real good but i thinks its bad. in the bathtub i put my croch under the fawcet and its great but i always feel gilty after. like i did

somthing bad. also my mom is getting
suspishus cause i take so many baths a day
and i ddidnt used to.

There are some that are completely
incomprehensible, and there are gems like
this one where the awful spelling is part
of the message. This is a public record of
a middle school kid discovering her crotch.
Half of this story is lost with any
editing.

For confession purists, you'll notice that
each confession has a number - completely
random - with which you can reference the
original, unmolested confession at
grouphug.us/book.

By the way, I've decided to make a few
personal confessions throughout this book:
smelling my own farts, so to speak.

Enjoy.

942931399

When I was a law student I drew up a contract transferring the immortal soul of the signatory to me. My colleague and I went to the liquor store and bought a fifth of Gordon's gin. We went out to the park and convinced a homeless guy to sign the contract in exchange for the gin.
I lost the contract a long time ago.
I am an atheist. I have no idea if he was.

Confess

674479928

When I was a young kid (but probably old enough to know better), for some unfathomable reason I took a shit on the carpet in the living room. I then told my mom the cat had done it. I'm still horrified to think that I actually did that.

Confess

815065711

I kind of miss high school. Isn't that pathetic?

Confess

667542951

I was waiting for my family to pick me up at my apartment for a big family dinner, but they were coming late. So I sat in front of the TV and started to channel surf. I was quickly distracted by a Wild On episode with Brooke Burke wearing nothing but a bikini in the Bahamas. After a few intense moments at staring at her perfect bare belly, I decided to whip out the old hand cream and pulled down my pants and began masturbating. It was pretty intense. I turned up the intensity trying to make sure that I came before the next commercial break. Then suddenly I heard the door jar wide open, and my

entire family walked in my living room, with my hand stuck on my peter. There was an initial shock of surprise, but I knew I couldn't stop, so I jizzed in front of my family. I ran back into the bathroom in front of their petrified faces, where I washed my hands and grabbed some toilet paper to clean up after myself.

Confess

174460748

When I was 12, I had a cockatiel named
Charlie. I liked to hold Charlie. I also
liked to sleep. The two didn't mix well
together. I fell asleep holding poor
Charlie and rolled over on him. He didn't
survive.

455826943

I am obsessed with watching how paper
towels soak up spilled liquids...it blows
my fucking mind.

563352918

My 1-year-old Newfoundland, Todd, loves to hump my wife. I actually get jealous because she laughs and finds it funny or cute. But at that moment all I can see is another male on my territory. How ridiculous is that?

Confess

293729543

I'm a woman and I work in a man's world as an electrician. I try to be badass like all the other guys, but I am so lonely in this shit town.

Confess

When I was in grade school I was always perfectly behaved. When the students would get in trouble we would have to "move our pen" on the bulletin board, and after that happened like 10 times they would call our parents.

Needless to say, I had never had to "move my pen" almost up until the end of the year. But one time, I forgot my homework at home, which would make me have to...but the teacher didn't make me. I reminded her that all the other students had to when they forgot their homework in the past, so she told me to "move my pen", and I did, and I flipped

out. I start crying and getting all emotional, and the teacher made me go sit outside in the hall.

Ironically after this one offense, the teacher called my parents cause I took it so poorly.

Confess

895072294

I've only cried at two movies...
It's a Wonderful Life, as one should and Home Alone...Why this movie, when so many more deserve it...kills me inside.

Confess

17

557109704

I am fat and ugly and no one could ever possibly find me at all attractive. I always bemoan the fact that everyone is so shallow, but even I find myself disgusting. Plus, I don't have a good personality either. I am a total loser. I am stupid, annoying, mean, and pathetic. Even if I weren't ugly, there is no reason that anyone would ever like me, but I still blame other people for being shallow.

742790773
My Weenie Is Tiny. *cries*

Confess

832236780
My girlfriend and I take turns reading
out loud to each other. The other night,
when we finished the last book we were
reading, I was in tears.
What a fucking pussy.

Confess

327661281

One time when I was in second grade we had to make kites. We all got to fly them outside and everyone was having lots of fun. I was running around with my mouth gaping open from laughing until suddenly I smacked into this other kid's face and inadvertently bit his eyeball out. There was blood everywhere and all the kids started crying. And so ended kite day.

Confess

496289646

I pretend I'm perfect but in fact I hate
myself for being such a jerk.

758464160

I think my parents are stupid. I'm
embarrassed that I'm their son, because
that means I'm probably stupid too. I
told my mother that.

528626929

I hate people who press the button at a crossing when the wait sign is already lit, I feel as though they are questioning my button pressing abilities. My friend did this earlier today and I hit him really hard. I don't think he deserved that.

275303023

One time I was backstage at a Dave Mathews show (who I can't stand) and I got so bored I went to the bathroom to masturbate. I thought I locked the door but I didn't and the drummer, Carter, walked in on me.

Confess

190262613

I had been a virgin until my late late teens, and my general lack of any sex drive didn't help the matter. A good friend of mine had recently become overly fed up with my supposed "weakness" one night while we were drinking at [his] house, so he proceeded to grab my cell phone when I wasn't paying attention, and called every female name I had in my phone book in alphabetical order (which I later found out included my best friend, neighbor, and my mother).

He managed to successfully invite over a friend of mine (at the time,) who was already mildly intoxicated. His full-blown

intentions were to get me laid, and he made this painfully obvious from the moment she set foot in the house. After an hour or so of flirting, massages, and eventual second base activity, he suggested that her and I move our fun to the spare bedroom across the hall. One thing led to another, and we ended up having sex.

Keeping in mind the common myth that male virgins tend to ejaculate rather quickly, I tried everything I could to keep my mind off of the pleasure I was experiencing. This ended up being a big mistake, as we found ourselves making drunken love for hours on end. Before we

knew it, the scent of coffee was filling the room, and I noticed there was a lot more light filling into the room through the window.

We both simultaneously figured that my instigating friend's father was waking up to go to work, and instantly jumped into a clothes-finding panic. Both of us were dressed and calm within roughly 30 seconds, and while I was putting on my shoes, his father slowly opens the door. We look up at him as sober and docile as we possibly could, and after staring at us for a moment, he says,

"I don't know what you two were doing in here, but you need to get the hell out

of this room."

As it turns out, I had just lost my virginity on the same bed that my (instigating) friend's grandmother spent her last month alive on. She passed away in her sleep less than 24 hours prior to the occasion.

360021994

One time while working at a restaurant, a woman and her daughter came in. Her daughter was wearing a big coat with a hood and I couldn't see her face. I grabbed a regular menu and a kid's menu and sat them down. Then the daughter took off her coat and it was a full-grown midget! She asked for a regular menu and I ran and got one, avoiding eye contact the rest of their meal.

Confess

190199034

I hate crabs, they scare the shit out of me. The animal, not the STD. I'd much rather have crabs, than actually deal with the crustacean crab.

371854250

My boyfriend just broke up with me, and now I'm hoping I get some horrible illness or suffer some huge tragedy so he'll pity me.

People think that I'm very sophisticated
and chic - men often compliment me by
telling me I'm beautiful and classy.
Here's a little secret: I pick my nose
and eat the boogers, I never wipe, I peed
in my very expensive, silk pants
yesterday, so I just splashed some talc
powder on the crotch and am wearing them
again today. My room is a mess. I stuff
my bra. I apply concealer very well in
order to hide the massive amounts of acne
and scars on my cheeks (ironically
enough, everyone always compliments me on
my "perfect" skin). I wear the same socks
(and go running in them) for sometimes a

week in a row. I have unruly, hairy pubic hair, which I only shave if I know that I'm going to get some action. I also have rather hairy nipples, which I also shave if an "occasion" is coming up. Oh yeah, did I mention that I pee in the steam room and public showers in my gym?

117529089

I "experimented" in college. I hooked up with this one guy online, walked over to his dorm, and we made out and groped each other. Then I sucked his cock. When I finished, he went to suck me and had a seizure. I haven't fooled around with anyone (men or women) since that. I heard he was okay later on, but he never called me back or anything.

Sometimes I wonder if he could have faked the seizure.

215931900

Once when I was a small child, I was
playing hide and go seek at a birthday
party, hid underneath a bed, and waited
for my cousin to come out of his hiding
place. After he did, I then grabbed a
metal baton and cracked him in the back
until he fell down.

Confess

8173657434

I threw rocks at a homeless guy once. I was young and wrong. If you are an ex-homeless guy, who once had rocks thrown at him, and who now is successful enough to get on the Internet, I'm sorry guy.

Confess

960924465

My cat was hit by a car. In my own garage.

Confess

524086943

I was addressing Christmas cards at work
the other day using my best cursive hand-
writing, and it looked really, really
good to me, and I started thinking of all
of these weird things, like people
receiving the cards looking at the hand-
writing and thinking it was the most
beautiful thing they'd ever seen, and
then coming and searching for me and then
I became famous for my hand-writing. I
felt really, really stupid for thinking
it, but it was nice at the same time. I'm
too embarrassed about it to tell my
friends, so I'm glad I found this site.

Confess

429254819

Once when I was driving home on the toll
road, I considered driving into the
barricade and killing myself just because
I wondered how many people/who from
school would show up at my funeral and be
emotionally devastated at my death.
It actually made me feel better about
myself.

Confess

933645720

I try to watch movies that make me cry.
Most of the time I don't. I just want to
feel human.

Confess

249135566

I made plans to travel across the country
and meet a man I am truly crazy about,
but something horrible happened that
prevented me from going. I have just
spent the last 4 hours trying to decide
what I'm more upset about. The horrible
thing, or missing out on spending a
weekend with this incredible man.
Oh, I also put barbeque sauce on just
about everything I eat.

728014205

One day while riding the elevator up to my office, I farted. It felt really hot, and when I sat down in my chair, I noticed a damp feeling in my pants. I walked to the restroom to check, and I had pooped in my pants. I threw my underwear away and cleaned up the best that I could. But because I had ridden the bus to work, I had to wait at the bus stop with other people and had a stain on the seat of my pants. I untucked my shirt, but it didn't cover it. When the bus finally came, I sat next to a bum so that if I stunk, the other people would hopefully think it was the bum who smelled like crap.

Confess

892735194

When I was 13 my grandfather caught me
rubbing one out and asked if he could
help. I said no thanks I've got it under
control. He shrugged and walked away.

Confess

393845560
I want to be somebody else.

Confess

403401007

One time I wanted a chicken parm sub so
badly that I cried.

Confess

565792187

My boyfriend cheated on me so I shaved
off my pubes and baked them in a cake.
Then watched when he scoffed the lot.

Confess

521167251

I am annoyed with my children tonight. I am annoyed that I don't have a thousand dollars to spend on Christmas this year, and instead, only three hundred. I am mad that I wrecked my hot rod, and now I am driving a piece of shit Ford Taurus rental car. I am sexually frustrated and I wish my husband would initiate sex sometimes so I don't have to beg for it. My feet hurt from new shoes. I wish I had big boobs. Okay that's enough. I'm feeling better already.

Confess

479228577

There's this one girl I asked to homecoming. I made my own fortune cookies and put a word in each, and strung them together. It spelled "Will you go to Homecoming with me?" But after lunch, I remembered that she was severely allergic to galvanized sugar, which was what I used to make them. Obviously she had some, cuz I found out later that she got her stomach pumped, but it was too late. Her liver couldn't process it, and now she needs a new liver. I would give her mine, but I don't think it's worth it. Then I can't go to Homecoming. Plus, we're probably not the same blood type so yea. Sorry though.

Confess

307218929

I love my girlfriend with all my heart.
But given a chance and some liquid
courage, there's a girl in Canada I'm
dying to get with, and also a girl
downstate I would kill to screw. Send me
to hell now, please, would you?

319347421

I wrote the original innuendo-laden London restaurant review which begins "When my boyfriend told me he wanted to take me up the Oxo Tower...", which is now circulating by email all over the world.

I feel a mixture of pride and shame, and I'm convinced my boss knows it was me. I'm too scared to bend down to the lower drawer of the filing cabinet in his presence.

970112446

I just swore on my kid that I'm not
sleeping with my friend - but I am, and
I might even leave my husband to be with
him. But probably not. I really hope the
baby wakes up in the morning.

Confess

316455666

I am a junior high band director and I hate my job. I used to be the director and music chairman for the district, but due to an exposed encounter a few years back, I lost my job. I engaged in an affair with an advisor for the band and shared a room on the spring trip. Unfortunately, one of the other advisors attempted to enter our room at night because of a student incident. This was the worst event of my life, next to losing a finger.

Confess

336633528

I happen to believe that you can be deeply in love with someone but have physical relations with other people on the side and that doesn't cheapen your love for the first person. But of course I can only admit that anonymously.

Confess

613677455

I have cheated on every boyfriend I've ever had.

Confess

567639337

Is it possible to marry someone and have
a good marriage after you have cheated on
them upwards of 7 times over 7 years and
never told them?

I hope so.

549605346

I stalk my friends on AOL Instant
Messenger with a secret screen name.

Confess

311922868

I'd like to think that I wouldn't fuck my
best friend's ex. I want to think that
I'm a good person and there's some things
you just don't do, no matter how
tempting.
But I will, the second I get the chance.

Confess

994921058

We teepeed a girl's house but got away
with it because her parents thought it
was the fault of disgruntled basketball
players. She is editor of the school
newspaper which wrote a critical expose
on the team.

Sometimes it would be nice if timing
were a person, so that we could hug it.

Confess

When I was younger, until I was about 16, when I got the shits with my parents I would lock myself in my room and turn off the TV aerial power supply off and leave them TV-less until I felt better. 5 years later I think about it and I still laugh.

Confess

373719337

I really liked this guy who was well out of my league. However he seemed to enjoy talking to me. We were at a party in winter, I went to leave, slipped on the icy step and hit my head. I was hurt but ok. I pretended to be completely knocked out so that he could carry me back into the house. It felt good.

Confess

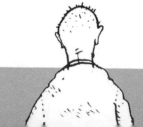

262699380

My wife is a good lay, and she thinks I am the best too. But I've found somebody else; our cleaning lady.

Confess

831599842

I'm seeing two girls, in somewhat long distance relationships, at the same time now. If I see each of them about half the time one should see a normal girlfriend, they just add up to one, and it's not so wrong... right?

Confess

210477254

I just found out I've been overpaid $800.
I'm not going to tell my boss I'm going
to just keep the money.

Confess

510451004

I've been feeding my cat expired cat
food.

Confess

417301935

I normally eat paper.

Confess

727144448

i just broke down in tears because the
hot water wasnt on and the shower was
cold.

  i think theres something wrong with me.

Confess

472435483

Sometimes I envision a tiny billy goat
who keeps watch over my hymen.

Confess

175536617

I don't use tampons . . . . . .
or pads . . . . . .
I use bread.

Confess

318534578

When I go into sports stores, I always
bend the visors of the baseball caps. I
hope my actions lessen the amount of
people walking around with ridiculous-
looking straight visors.

Confess

192928062

When I was a kid, I found some beer in the woods that someone had hidden there. I drank two of them and peed in the bottles and put the caps back on. The later that day, my friend called me and invited me to go party in the woods with him and a bunch of other kids, he said they had beer.

Confess

406429093

I have intentionally urinated on someone before.

Confess

450933231

I eat pills I find on the floor.

Confess

988070868

I hate taking a shit and everything about it. It's time consuming, the buildup's uncomfortable, and it's annoying to clean myself afterwards.

I take Immodium on a regular basis so I only have to poop twice a week.

153506694

i hate madonna's fake-ass british accent.

581241072

When I was 11, for a cheap thrill, I cut a football in half and filled it with hair mouse and then shagged it.

Having now had sex I realised that I was way off the mark and all it did was give me a penis irritation which I told my mum about. Leaving the detail of the ball fucking incident, obviously.

I still think the reason why my pubes are so wirey is because I styled them at such a young age.

Confess

497546050

Im from London. I pretend to hate
northerners, but I secretly find mouthy
northern bints incredibily attractive.
I also hate Irish people.

733035671

i shagged the fittest bird in school last
weekend. No one belives me and she hasn't
been here all week to back me up.

449307741

I like to keep friends who are uglier than me, fatter than me, or dumber than me so I look really good next to them.

Confess

699802122

I'm a female and I shave my knuckles.

Confess

201043304

I went to a Kenny Rogers concert and he was throwing Frisbees into the audience. He only threw the Frisbees to the women, so I was pissed off I didn't get one. I don't know why. I only went to the concert to hear him sing "The Dukes Of Hazzard" theme song, and he didn't even sing that. That show was such a rip off.

Confess

626043128

I stopped reading Fast Food Nation half way through because I do enjoy the McDonald's Sausage and Egg Muffin breakfast and, well, ignorance is bliss.

121285088

Today is pajama day in the office and I have no underwear on.

Confess

454648560

Well...its kind of hard to say this...I don't know...it was a weird time. Well here's how it goes. I was walking down a street one day and found this muskrat that couldn't walk. So I picked it up and brought it home and started caring for it. I fed it pizza. We watched TV...and I named it Henry. He became my best friend and he died yesterday. I don't want to believe he is dead, he's still on my chair! I'm just going to leave him there...

Confess

435424691

I hooked up with my ex-boyfriend 6 months after we broke up when I was really drunk.

Thing is, I woke up in his flatmate's bed and had no idea how I got there, having peed all over his carpet. Then another flatmate walked in on us attempting to have sex doggy-style.

Not my greatest morning, I'll willingly admit.

Confess

614707639

I got home one day to find that the cat had crapped all over the carpet. there was no-one else in, so I made it look like I'd never come in and I went straight out. I didn't come back til I know my flatmate was home. She told me how she'd come home and had to clean it all up and I said "Aw, you poor thing, having to do that on your own, I would have helped if I'd been here".

N.B. I have used this tactic on more than one occasion.

Confess

324689547

I masturbated on a London Underground
District Line train somewhere between
Barking and Upminster.

Confess

758432913

I think deep down I believe that I'll be
able to trick God into believing that I'm
actually a good person when the time
comes.

Confess

16580231

I feel guilty and sometimes ashamed about
how much money my family has and the
privileges that has afforded me.

Confess

Once when I was at the cinema I needed to have a piss half way through the film. Because I didn't want to go to the toilet, I pissed in an empty Coke cup and put it in the cup holder on the armrest. It was actually quite a shit film. I don't know why I couldn't just have gone to the toilet and missed a few minutes of the film. But doing the wrong thing gave me a buzz.

Confess

399282639

I once was waiting for an elevator and when the doors opened, there was a baby there on the floor of the elevator in the car seat. Instead of taking the baby out, I instead waited for the doors to close and take the baby to another floor.

Confess

186791769

A girl at work once whispered to me "come to the paper room so we'd be alone"...I looked at her and asked "why?"

Confess

812061834

I just ended a phone conversation with my boss by saying "peace."

Confess

183365722

I really wish I was in the witness protection program. Not because I'm in trouble, but because I'd like to start over with a new name, new job, new life. A fresh start.

There should be a company that provides this service.

Confess

873966489

Sometimes I wish that I was retarded and act on all my impulses freely.

Confess

139879104

I secretly pray to God just so I have a backup.

Confess

73

58393391

I slept with one person in my entire
life, and got an STD. I guess it's better
than a kid.

Confess

262682896

If I hadn't grown up in society I would
want to touch people all the time all
over.

Confess

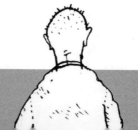

129891320

One of my better friends at my university
has this habit of petting his sideburns,
and I swear to God, if I see him do it
again, I'll shave them off.
It drives me nuts.

Confess

918256637

I'm jealous of her, that's why we aren't
friends.

Confess

345542986

I fucking hate eating pomegranates because they're such a god-damned hassle. I used to eat them, and for some reason I stopped. But now, I remember why. Such a god-damned hassle.

 Confess

787222536

i went to a tori amos cd signing at borders while i was in london. i am such a freak.

Confess

625031247

I like to draw on my body, it relaxes me.
I do it in spots where my clothes cover
it. People think it is odd that a thirty-
year-old male still uses the back of his
hand to write reminders and numbers. If
they only saw what going on my arms,
stomach and legs.

Confess

164038267

I still like playing with LEGOS.

Confess

554918579

Back in elementary school we were playing kickball as a class. One guy that I hated had just kicked the ball and was running towards first, admiring his shot when he ran right into the soccer goal post. The resulting "clang" was the best sound I have ever heard in my life, and I burst out laughing. My classmate yelled at me saying "it isn't funny."

Actually, it was. Very much so.

Confess

969368653

I like to build elaborate forts in my living room and just sit in them for hours on end. I'm 32.

365927710

I don't know why, but every time I see
someone leave their convertible top down
on their car, I have the sudden urge to
put something in it. I mean I will
rummage through my car to find something
to put in there.

The other day I had my fiancé put my
iced tea in the cup holder.

One time it was a half eaten peach.
It's a fetish. I don't know where it
comes from.

605488322

I work as a contractor in London. Each
time I work in a new company I defacate
on the floor daily for the first couple
of weeks. I find it
quite exhilarating. I have never been
caught which provides a real buzz. I just
can't stop myself.

Confess

635663605

One of my favorite hobbies is to dress up in designer clothes and do my hair and makeup. Then I put on a baseball cap and sunglasses and go grocery shopping pretending to be a famous celebrity who just wants to lead a normal life.

Confess

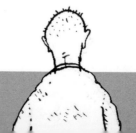

193128551

Some days I want to kill myself but I want to make it look like my neighbor Ted did it. He won't give me back my lawn mower and I hate him. I hope he gets the chair.

Confess

1078988

I pull the nose hairs out of my boogers before I eat them. Because eww; who wants to eat nose hairs?

Confess

180146774

When I'm getting ready in the mornings, I like to moan and shudder and squirt out the toothpaste on to my brush as if I'm blowing my load.

Confess

616305961

I have a velvet robe and smoke a pipe w/ bubbles I feel unstoppable when I wear it.

Confess

798461257

I've stopped resisting so much. As a result, I find the world less important and more pleasant.

Confess

291497973

I am a girl who refuses to shave my moustache off, I feel like it is a part of me   - People tell me I look like Tom Selleck.

Confess

85

143731580

When I was younger, I thought if you had braces and glasses then you were so awesome and hot . . . I was a very jealous little kid.

Confess

531321235

I'm 20 years old, and just figured out that Kanga and Roo from Winnie the pooh spell out the word "kangaroo"

Confess

835503949

I've always believed in trying everything
at least once. I liked anchovies on my
pizza. I didn't like getting fucked in
the ass by a huge black guy.

Confess

410088153

I am very afraid that I will die someday,
and when my parents come to clean out my
room, they'll find my vibrator and my
memory will be tainted forever.
Unfortunately, I don't know what to do
about this, and I sure as hell am not
giving up my vibrator.

Confess

Whenever I call someone on the phone, I write out what I am going to say. If I am alone, I practice saying it before I call, even if it's just something really short and simple. I even write in some "um's" so it doesn't sound scripted. Sometimes I write one version for if a person answers and a different version for if I get the voice mail. If I haven't written a voice mail version and I get the voice mail, I have to hang up and call back later after I have written a voice mail version.

When there is a voice mail system that allows you to listen to your message

before sending, I usually erase and re-record the message at least 5 times before sending.

Confess

435254832
After years of contemplation, I really think that I may be an atheist. It scares me a lot.

Confess

855692379

I have a mitten phobia. Anytime anyone
wears knit mittens, and tries to touch my
arm or any part of my exposed skin with
them, I freak out and run. I just don't
like the feeling, and something about the
way mittens look creep me out.

Confess

650095414

I'm 19 now. When I was young, maybe
around 18, I used to put on a ski mask,
gloves, a long-sleeved t-shirt, jeans,
socks, underwear, and boots, and go out
into my backyard to kill bees. I would go
over to my mom's lavender bushes and clap
my hands on the bees for about an hour
every day.

God I hate bees.

165694495

I hate the colour pink - salmony pink
probably the worst.

Confess

572359945

I wish that Dr. Phil would kill himself.
That would really fuck up the Dr. Phil
crowd.

Confess

602623850

I dumped my boyfriend over the weekend. I
should have done it earlier but I wanted
to see what he would get me for
Christmas.

Confess

506548433

There is a guy in the office who always,
without fail, gives me the shooter salute
and clicks his cheeks while winking, I
would like to snap off his finger.

Confess

I have no faith in the human race. My job is in tech support. Those stories about people using their CD-ROM drives as cup holders and not knowing where the "any" key is are true. By true I mean one of these happens to me on a daily basis. One out of 20 people I talk to has to be told how to type the "@" symbol in their e-mail address, or how to shut down their computer. I had to explain to one guy what an electrical outlet was. Do you know what this means?? This means that an average of 5% of the population barely has the knowledge to get out of bed in the morning. I get paid 7 dollars an

hour, and sometimes I get calls from network administrators at companies like Hewlett Packard. I am not kidding. This is not a joke. The world lays in the hands of complete morons.

535221899

I recently bought a new car. I have been saving up for ages. I doubled my working week and got a night shift at Tesco's. It's a really nice K reg Nissan and I loved it.

I went into town one day to meet a friend and hang out. I parked in the local car park where it wasn't busy on a Wednesday lunch. My friend pulls up in the space next to mine in a brand new Peugot 206. I secretly am in love with this car, which is why it hurts so much. On our way into the centre, I slyly keyed the side of his car. It was the whole length of the passenger door.

The next day I found myself in the car park at Tesco's just before I was supposed to be working. I see a relatively new Golf GTi. I could not help it but scratch the car again, this time along the whole car.

I have no regrets except for the fact that I am 39 and 40 in one month and I haven't keyed more things in the past - be them cars or not.

645598619

One time my friend got really drunk and passed out on the sofa. He had pissed me off earlier so I farted in his open mouth while he was passed out. He deserved it.

Confess

651119810

I can't stand people named Melissa. They are all the same.

Confess

326545389

I hate flies. A day that starts with killing one is a good day. As a child I tore their wings off, and liked seeing them that way. Sometimes I have sex with my husband so he'll shut up, go to sleep, and leave me alone.

Confess

74120795

I hate George W. Bush more than just about anyone on earth because he's so fucking stupid and is screwing up the world...but I secretly think he's kind of cute.

Confess

393778192

I get girls in the sack by acting like a
righteous homosexual who's "saving
himself". When they "find out" that it's
them I want to "lose it with", they
totally fall for it. I then resume acting
gay and ask them not to say anything.
They never do.

Confess

751213806

I'm 16. When I was little I used to catch birds with my bare hands. My grandma says I'd follow them for hours, until they got used to me being there, then I'd pounce on them. I never meant to hurt them, but I killed a couple.

Confess

In France I got sick of people jumping my queue, and finally lost it with an old guy who inserted himself slowly 2 places in front of me very slowly. I yelled at him, humiliated him in front of everyone, insulting him (all this in decent French) very strongly, and wouldn't listen to his pathetic attempts to explain...that he was blind and unable to see anything more than a few inches in front of his face. Which is why he was hanging around where he thought the line ended.

Confess

596545787

At around age 1 1/2, I've been told that I was busted, not once, but twice, sucking and chewing on slugs from my mom's garden.

467357274

I tripped a mentally ill kid.

579266971

When I was about 8 I was at Sefton Park
Lake in Liverpool in England. We were
throwing stones at the swans in the lake.
None of us really intended to hit one,
well I certainly didn't. But I did hit
one, right on the head and it died
instantly. I ran home crying and have
never really forgiven myself.

940281357

I press the "door close" button on the elevator when I see people running for it.

Confess

726365375

I lived next door to a deaf kid when I was 14. Every Saturday at like 7 in the morning, he'd go in his backyard and beat on a metal pole with a baseball bat. After 2 months, I had had enough, so I jumped the fence and kicked his ass.

Confess

922096479

I used to catch flies in a plastic bag,
freeze them into deep sleep, then super
glue their feet to post-it notes
airplanes. Watched as they woke up and
the planes flew away....

Confess

57002981

One time I pissed off a 5 story roof onto
a couple that was making out on the
sidewalk below. I was very drunk but I
always felt guilty about that.

Confess

593505996

I killed a mouse once by throwing it into a campfire and kicking it back in whenever it tried to run out.

Confess

325319493

I write really, really horrible gay fan fiction about the X-Men. Literally, I write homosexual fan fiction about Wolverine having sex with as many male characters as possible, and it's really poorly written.

And my brother helps me write some of it.

Confess

755890792

I eat my own cum after masturbating,
every single time.

951257987

I wear a cowboy hat to work just to try
and get this girl to suck my willy.

Confess

284978120

I was baking cookies in the oven, nude.
When I bent over to pick up the tray my
testicles fell onto the cookie sheet.
I can no longer achieve orgasm unless I
feel extreme heat but I told everyone it
was because of cancer.

I feel so bad.

Confess

93778824

I once begged for extra money on Regent
Street, despite the fact that I had a
full time job and earned enough to rent a
flat and get
wasted all the time. I used to beg during
London rush hour, collecting up to 40
quid an hour. This went on for months,
until a bloody Sun journalist wrote about
fake begging...

Confess

952061919

My tastes in pornography are becoming
less and less socially acceptable.

Confess

957645445

I once watched my mum get dressed by
putting strategically placed mirrors
throughout the corridor all the way to my
room.

Confess

855269394

My mother had an old "massaging device" when I was little. I thought it was just a back massager. It wasn't shaped like a penis or anything. It just had this big motor with a shaft sticking out of it which was a little wider than my thumb (I have big hands) and about 4 inches long. I'd turn it on and hold it very tightly, trying to make it hold still. Sometimes, I'd stick it in my mouth and clench my teeth on it. I liked how it vibrated my head.

About 10 years later, I suddenly remembered that 'massaging device'. OMG...

my mother had a dildo-like device, left
it out all the time, and let me chew on
it.

505976245

Masturbating to Internet porn (I'm a girl) with one hand and eating Cheetos with the other, I suddenly realized there was no way I could save the mouse...never have I felt so pathetic.

591181852

Sometimes when I masturbate, my father pops into my head. I am totally grossed out and have to stop. I wish this wouldn't happen.

Confess

374803314

I secretly wish that men I knew
masturbated while thinking of me.

Confess

396938617

The first time I ever masturbated was in
the shower on a Sunday morning. The
second time was in the church bathroom
about an hour later.

Confess

369480504

I really enjoy squeezing out ingrown hairs... This is the main reason I get my bikini line waxed, for some reason I always get more there.

Confess

397633263

When I'm out running, I secretly feel superior to all of the people who walk by me. I like to believe that they know I'm better than them too.

Confess

241677804

I sniff my dad's underwear. I'm a guy.

Confess

415590019

Sometimes when I'm shaving, I will purposely not shave between my upper lip and nose. This leaves a good amount of shaving cream on that part of my face, which forms a Hitler-esque mustache... and then I walk around my dorm room naked, yelling "seig heil!"

Confess

235172338

I have just recently dropped my guitar pick in the toilet and I have this very bad habit of putting it into my mouth whenever I have to stop and read the music and I don't think I can stop.

Confess

937205178

I'm a 79-year-old grandmother of two, I regularly sit near to people on the bus who I find attractive and purr at them. This does include females.

Confess

423006690

I had sex with Dustin Diamond (Screech from "Saved by the Bell") - no joke.

865732533

My life is over. Three days ago I awoke from a sexy dream to find myself having sex with my brothers feet. He was awake and he just said go back to bed. I know he's going to tell dad.

585546211

I like to masturbate while driving, its like killing 2 birds with one stone.

Confess

786078571

Nearly every night I sneak out of our Amish community to read grouphug in the library.

Confess

178205418

When I was a kid, I thought I was the reincarnation of Jesus. Every once in awhile, I still do.

Confess

868557309

All the times I've ever had sex in my life were for the purpose of burning calories, whether I liked the person or not.

Confess

327885315

I wish I had a stalker who was obsessed with me. That would totally turn me on.

Confess

386919418

I buy CDs that I think will look impressive in my collection. I want to give the impression that I am "musically educated." I'm such a tool.

Confess

920206877

I was feeling a little "lonely" last night. I thought I would feel better if I put the vacuum cleaner hose on my penis. I did feel better last night, but my girlfriend came home and saw me. She started crying. She just doesn't understand about the vacuum thing. Now I feel guilty about it.

I cheated my way through college using Cliff notes and copying off of other people's tests.

I did more work finding random books to copy my master's thesis than probably would have taken to just do the thesis myself.

My resume is total bull shit, except for the fact that I do have a master's degree (which was described above), and I use friends who lie for me as references and make me look better than I am.

I am seriously under-qualified for the position I have at work.

There are people with higher education

than me, work harder than me, who make tens of thousands of dollars less than I do at this company.

I can't say I really feel that bad about all of this, because I'm a really good "people person." I've bull-shitted my way through the majority of my life, and I'm a very successful business person - at least everyone else thinks so.

I have an office full of books I've only skimmed enough though to be able to talk about them for a short time.

I take the maximum allowable charitable donation for church on my taxes, but I do not donate because I know it's something

that doesn't raise a "red flag" with the IRS.

I feel like no one even knows me, but it's too late to do anything about it.

I will probably marry my long time girlfriend and have children and raise them to be upstanding citizens - "because look how far that got daddy."

Life is what you make of it I guess.

I often wonder what it is like to be real.

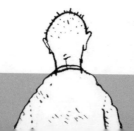

I made some marijuana brownies one day, and when I left them to cool my mother came home from work and ate almost half of them. She had never been stoned before, and when she got the massive hit she curled up in a ball on the ground in her room, screaming that she was dieing. She made me write her a new will, in which the goldfish would inherit the house. I never told her that it was brownies that made her so sick, and she's still convinced it was a bad oyster she had for lunch.

Confess

I go to school with a blind girl. I made friends with her, but now I kinda regret it. She's always asking me to walk her to class, always calling me, and always asking me to take her everywhere. It's kind of an inconvenience for me but I always feel bad when I tell her I can't. But inside I just wanna yell "Don't you have any other friends? I don't wanna be your personal assistant, damn it! Fuck Off!" What makes it worse is that she doesn't wanna help herself. She likes being completely dependent on others and it pisses me off! Somebody asked her once if she would ever consider getting a dog

to guide her and she said no really fast.
I feel really bad for thinking like this
but, that quickly subsides...

Confess

361600376
I check out fat ugly men so they don't
feel so ugly...

 Confess

At college I grab girls rear-ends and say, "Hey Jessica."

Then apologize and say they looked really like my best girl friend from behind - And get away with it all the time.

883431069

I once stole a car, broke all the windows, and left it in a parking garage. I gave the man I stole the car from a description of the person who I said was trying to open his vehicle. He called the Police and they arrested the person I had described. This other person was my uncle who had just been released from prison and was on 10 month probation for grand theft auto. I don't know why I did this, I regret it, and no one knows.
My uncle is still in jail.

Confess

553528919

In 5th grade this kid I didn't like had
broken his foot. I told him I was going
to step on it and he said I wouldn't. I
stomped on it as hard as I could. He was
so delirious from the pain that he told
the principal it was the kid on the other
side of him in line. The other kid was
suspended.

Confess

694852420

I had my 13 year-old dog put to sleep because it was really starting to bug me but I convinced my wife and the vet that it was sick.

Confess

550864131

I played solitaire while my gf masturbated over the phone. I'm not secretly gay or anything, I had just finished already. And I won the game. :D

Confess

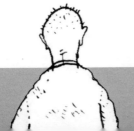

580810347

My flatmate comes home with the really slutty girls that have been around the block more times than a kid who has just got a new bike

I decided to prick holes in half of his rubbers. U can call it Russian Roulette Condoms

I've never felt so satisfied

Confess

697864276

I live with my flatmate. He really annoys
me sometimes (he picks scabs off his neck
and forehead and stealthily puts them in
his mouth, but I can see it out of the
corner of my eye)

Anyway, he pisses me off, and I wonder
how it would turn out if we got in a
fight. I think about this too much, and
the other day I saw him carrying a TV up
the stairs and he was really struggling,
because it was heavy. I didn't help him,
but when he went out of the room, I
picked it up to see how heavy it was, to
get an idea of how strong he is.

432563812

This boy fell asleep in my art class yesterday so my friends and I put crayons up his nose.

He was pretty mad when he woke up so I apologized and even made him an "I'm sorry I put crayons in your nose while you were sleeping" tape.

The truth is, I'm not really that sorry, and I'd definitely do it again.

Confess

534015472

My butt is always itchy. Sometimes I go
to the bathroom at work just to scratch
it. It's not a little scratch either. I
scratch right up to the anus. Maybe I
have worms.

Confess

791414137

I'm crazy about this guy who lives
upstairs but he's a freak who hates women
and likes kung fu.

But he does this really cool thing with
his eyebrow.

Confess

685854183

I started eating with my left hand (even
though I am right-handed) just because
the guy I like is left-handed.

Confess

180766939

I wish my loving, caring, honest
boyfriend would just fuck off.

Confess

326590853

Another day.
Love is hard to find.
Every day I feel sadder.
Xylophones are my only friend.
Boobies I have not seen.
Relief I have not felt.
As if that wasn't sad enough.
Kissing isn't my thing.

Confess

139

743194657

I feel like throwing up when I kiss my girlfriend.

I almost did last night.

Confess

264606956

My friend and I had some weed but no paper to roll a joint with, so we used the page from my Bible that had John 3:16 in it.

I'm going to hell for that.

Confess

880163330

I'm 18 and male, and I have been sleeping
with my best friend's father for four
years. He even married my mom just to be
with me every chance he could get. I'm
better at giving head than her.

191108508

I really am not attracted to my
girlfriend anymore. I stay with her
because of the dog.

Confess

121285088

I'm 17 and I still use the small spoons.

Confess

194206869

I fucked up the rent money this month
buying heroin, porn, and a slew of anal
beads and vibrators. Now I have to take
one of those short-term high interest
loans online just so I won't be evicted.
I am so damn stupid I really don't
deserve to have my own place.

Confess

150636360

Sometimes I eat so many Skittles, and I eat them so fast that I lacerate my gums. I'll go to brush my teeth afterwards but I have to stop because all this blood is pouring out of my mouth. Also I get a bad stomach ache and I have crazycrazycrazy dreams. I have another pack of Skittles in my pocket and I'm going to go eat them right now.

313217326

I love porno like a fat kid loves cake.

Confess

376989132

I may pretend to be interested in someone's religion just to make out with them.

Confess

966352329

When no one is looking, I eat the pineapples at work. I love the pineapples. It's not like many people order pineapples on their pizza anyway. I also eat the pepperonis...lots of pepperonis.

Confess

856247335

I secretly still am addicted to Hanson, even though I'm a hardcore emo kid.

Confess

146

361673160

I need to get this out. Years ago I took
LSD with a good friend. I ended up
thinking he was a space alien and beating
[him] up with a baseball bat, which I
thought was like a Star Wars light sabre.
He ended up in the ER and took another
three weeks in hospital to recover. It
freaked me out and I never had the
courage to tell him it was me.

147

Back in college, I had this pal who had a
really annoying neighbor. She had this
ugly-assed dog she supposedly paid a lot
of money for, and all night it would just
bark, bark, and bark. My pal had these
plans to shoot the dog, but one night we
got really stoned and decided to steal
the dog and hold it for ransom (you know
those pot dreams). We stole the dog, but
neglected to say, tell her or leave a
note. I kept the dog at my place, and he
actually turned out to be a pretty cool
little dog. Well, the neighbor called the
police, and things got hot an heavy so I
sort of had to keep the dog at my place

for a while... and then weeks turned into years...

Last week, he died at age 15 (we think). He's lived with me since I was 21, moved across the US twice, and been a loving and devoted pet to my two sons. I told my wife I found him in the street when we were dating and sort of kept up the lie since then.

I have no idea if I did the right thing or not, but I miss my little buddy so much.

866300444

When I was 23 years old, I got drunk, stripped completely naked, and climbed out onto the railing of my townhouse balcony at 3 AM or so. In the townhouse next to mine lived a married couple about fifteen years older than me, and the woman was hot, hot, hot. I assumed correctly that they did not bother to lock their balcony door (neither did I), so I climbed over the dividing wall and then went right into their bedroom. Both of them were naked and asleep on top of the sheets. The husband was snoring so loudly, I could have belched the alphabet and they wouldn't have heard it. I walked around

to the lady's side and admired her for a
while, then I leaned down and sniffed her
skin (and hairy places) as closely as I
could. Then, at a loss for what to do
next, I simply took one of their pillows
and climbed back over to my own balcony.
They never knew a thing about it, and we
continued for several more years to have
polite neighborly relations. I still have
that pillow in my bed, as a matter of
fact.

380172758

I can't socialize without being drunk.
Everybody knows this about me though.
Maybe it's not a confession.

Confess

661039935

when i was in london i told my old school
friends that i had been working in
jerusalem but i had really been in paris,
france.

Confess

my uni friends are lazy idiot dickheads
with no social skills. they really piss
me off. i hate seeing them at uni, but am
stuck with them now.

they think i have a grumpy disposition,
but really its just them.

Confess

153

702463450

I have your property and have no
intentions of giving it back in one
piece. That being said, it is safe to
assume that it is in several pieces.
That's right, I cut it into several
pieces and hid it so no one can find it
except me. This is what you get for
stealing what was rightfully ours. Payback
is a bitch, isn't it?

Confess

154

699622873

Once in college my buddies and I got a letter in our mailbox that was addressed to some people down the street. It looked like a card, and we were feeling like jerks, so we steamed it open over a teakettle. It said "Congratulations on Your Marriage. Have a Great Life Together. - Aunt Judy." She also included $200 cash. My buddies and I took the money, and threw away the card. I'm honestly, truly ashamed of myself and it makes me sick to think about it.

847385072

Today, while drinking at happy hour at an undisclosed chain restaurant, a disgruntled psychotic patron threw a bar stool at the bartender. In the shuffle he lost his prescription barbiturates. I stole them and just swallowed one. I hope he didn't need those pills to stop him from killing someone.

579148740

I'm going to steal my roommate's Dilbert
calendar tonight. I feel sort of bad
about doing this, but she has it coming
to her.

Confess

202726686

When I was about 13 my friend and I snuck out of our houses one night and got loaded off cheap vodka I stole from my dad. We roamed the streets yelling at passers by and eventually made our way into one of those Arabian all night convenience stores. With the liquor in us, we were feeling pretty daring and decided to rob the store of several bags of barbeque charcoal. For what purpose, I don't know. So here we are walking around, completely drunk with bags of charcoal and nothing to do...so we start hurling the coal at cars driving by while hiding in some bushes. Eventually we get

bored of that and start throwing the entire bags. Well we had some good luck with this for a while, but then we threw one that landed right through the windshield of this shitty old Nissan or some kind of shit car like that. A couple of big African men got out and chased us through the woods. After about 5 minutes of running, both of us were out of breath and the angry black gentlemen caught up with us and thoroughly beat the living shit out of us and stole our money. When my mom woke me up for school the next morning I explained all the bruises by telling her I had fallen down the stairs during the night and accused her of being

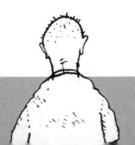

a bad mother for not hearing it. She felt
bad and went out and bought me breakfast
from McDonalds, and a VHS copy of
"Raiders Of The Lost Ark." I feel
horrible about it in retrospect, but
sometimes I'll be sitting in my desk at
work and just burst into a maniacal fit
of laughter thinking about the incident.

Confess

465737975

Last month my car broke down at the store, I didn't feel like walking, so I stole one of those handicapped motorized shopping carts and rode it home. Then I sold it on eBay.

Confess

310046853

There's a guy at work who keeps candy in a little dish on his desk. Whenever I pass his cubicle and he's not there, I take a handful of that shit.

Confess

245481294

I think the girl I slept with last night stole my left shoe. I wish I had asked her what her name was.

Confess

961762807

The term flatmate makes me so mad i punch holes in my walls

Confess

619427462

I just wanked and wiped my hands on my flatmates chair. My other flatmate then preceded to unknowinly sit in it, pretending to be my annoying flatmate.

814619869

One time my little brother was pestering
the hell out of me and he would not
cease, so I bit my arm as hard as I could
and blamed the teeth-marks on him. He sat
in the corner for the rest of the while I
played with his He-Man action figures.

Confess

342249937

I hid a magnetic strip thing deep inside my dad's wallet after he pissed me off one day. He gets stopped at every store for setting off the alarm and can't figure out why. It's been 9 months of this. I'm starting to feel bad about it...

Confess

413857026

I want to be the better person after this break up, but only so I can rub her face in it.

Confess

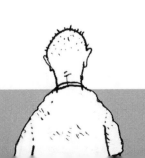

325650418

So constipated.

Confess

660818491

i am a male, yet i never pee standing up.
i just never sem to have got the hang of
it..

my flatmates think i am the best
flatmate ever as i never leave the toilet
seat up...

i can never tell them..

Confess

733864076

There is a retarded guy who sometimes
gets on the bus I take to uni, and I sit
in the single seats just so he won't sit
next to me. I feel like shit when I do
that.. but I'm always gonna do it.

Confess

114781373

I work at a hair salon and I save the
hair of a particular woman whose hair I
style. I keep the hair in jars that I
store in my basement.

Confess

280520259

I made a really amazing roast beef dinner
on Sunday, and I didn't want to share it
with my flatmate, so I hid the leftovers
at the bottom of the fridge so I could
eat the rest of it when she wasn't
around.

I do this sort of thing a lot.

I feel really mean about not sharing
roast potatoes and boiled carrots, but I
still don't want her to have any.

821903745

I work with this kid called chris and i cant stand him, he reckons hes a proper south london gangster like hes in so solid, but really hes a little fasico

Confess

429022226

Where do all the nice men in London hide? I only ask because I've never met one. And I confess that foreigners and asylum seekers don't count as people, let alone men.

Confess

768031670

I had to kick a couple of kids out of my building last night; they were trespassing and spraying shitty tags all over the place. I remember doing all that stuff not so long ago (I'm only 23) so I just kicked them out rather than call the police which is what my neighbours would do.

Anyway, three of these kids were white and one was black. The black guy starts shouting that I'm a racist. Now this annoyed me. I'm a total fucking liberal, I grew up in easily the most racially diverse area in Britain, and I don't even really *see* what colour people are. It just doesn't occur to me (And anyway, I

170

was chucking out the white boys as well).

This happened a few months ago as well, a group of kids had got into a fight on a bus and as the police were kicking them off, the black kids among the group were saying "Yeah, fucking police are all racist". Admittedly, the London police are institutionally racist, but why do these thug kids use racism as a crutch to justify their lack of respect for others? Freeloading of any kind annoys me, and this kind of cultural tarring is just fucked up. Fucking kids.

So, I guess I'm confessing to being upset that this kid called me a racist, in case you were wondering.

Confess

610824969

I have just bet my mate £500 that I will beat him at the London Marathon. I feel dirty.

Confess

558126471

i shagged my mates bird. she had massive tits. great fun.

Confess

172

606833453

The first time I drank vodka me and my
mate didn't realise the concept of
spirits - on the tube on the way to a
party on the other side of london I
projectile vomited over a sweet little
old lady through my hands.I managed to
spray her head to well heeled toe while
only getting a smatter on myself - being
as enebriated as I was I asked her for
her tissue which she gave me (in shock)
from her puke-filled handbag - sorry!

Confess

802354389

I wish to confess to having had full-blown penetrative sex on the number 13 bus on the way to uni one day. I told my flatmates this in a drunken mess earlier this week and they were all shocked for some reason.

They have conductors on some London buses who you either buy tickets off or show your travelcard to. We were sat upstairs at the front, and the conductor never bothered to ask for our ticket for some reason...

I have no recollection of the lecture that I was going to on the bus. But the journey was memorable.

Confess

222332766

I support a football team in London that is currently performing extremely well and is actually one of the most exciting teams throughout Europe at the moment.

However, I do not like the manager of the club and as a result I am always whinging and criticising him, thus really annoying my fellow fans.

I know it makes me look foolish but I just cannot help myself with my constant moaning. I think I need help really but cannot bring myself to admitting it to my fellow fans.

306268097

I'm from the U.S. but I worked in London for a summer during college. I opened a bank account and right before I left for home, I overdrafted 100 pounds from the bank. A month later I got a letter from the bank saying that I would be arrested at customs if I ever tried to re-enter the U.K. I could not possibly care less.

Confess

259741130

in uni, i kept a toilet roll by the bed
to mop up frequent and furious wanks.
being lazy, after each deed, i'd just
chuck the "sopping" tissue down the side
of the bed and forget about it. on the
day left uni, a few friends helped me
move out of the apartment - they pulled
my bed away from the wall and to my
horror, loads of crusty used tissues were
stuck to the wall revealing my nightly
deeds. i'll never live it down....i'm
such a wanker

Confess

29550525

Me and a mate at Uni worked out the fuse
box for our house. We turned off the
power points for the room of this
annoying groover in the house and
listened as he came in and turned on his
stereo to play his iritating music, and
then heard the frustration and finally
panic of his frantically switching it on
and off. Then we turned the lights out of
the room of a german bloke upstairs. He
was useless with girls and finally had
one in his room, but he wasn't quite in
the zone with her and the lights going
off wrecked his chances. I think she felt
like she was being watched.

Confess

325748476

I have always peed while I take a shower,
and i sometimes masturbate too. But I
make sure to wash it off. I think its ok
for me to do it, but not ok for others.

Im in uni now, and someone told me that
people do that in the showers, I just
looked at him like he was sick.
hehe. sucker.

738922083

When I as about 13 I shagged the gap between two of the seat cushions of my mums new settee. It was just at the right height. I cleaned it all up.

Confess

61132269

A friend and I started a rumour at school that a teacher shagged sheep. Everyday to his face, behind his back, all the time we would make Baaa noises, like a sheep. It got to the stage the whole school would make sheep noises at him and to each other. After 6 months he started to cry when we did it. Apparently he moved schools and the rumor followed. 10 years on and people still do it. I would just like to say sorry Horace. Baaa.

399041766

I once shagged a girl with a lazy eye, we were both drunk and she showed me her chest, i made her bark like a dog, i told her that i would shag her so hard that i would give her another lazy eye, i dont think it went well with her, too bad she didnt look that bad, except for the whole lazy eye thing;-P

Confess

25254972

I shagged my cousin when I was drunk. Worse, I went back and did it again a week later. I know it's legal but try telling our dads that.

Confess

881490672

A few months ago I made it my mission to wipe my knob on the driver's side door handle of every silver Audi TT I saw. I started off in a carpark in Manchester. I racked up quite a few but had to stop as the weather made it too hazardous.

Confess

13777899

i once dressed my dog up in the Manchester United kit and put a poster of Devid Beckhams face over her head. I then tried having sex with my dog while having the fantasy of having sex with David Beckham. She bit me.

Confess

I am honestly afraid that, in the end, a mildly perverse Web site and this book might be considered my major contributions.

I confess ...

Confess